I AND I
BOB MARLEY

I AND I

BOB MARLEY

by **Tony Medina**

illustrated by **Jesse Joshua Watson**

LEE & LOW BOOKS INC.
NEW YORK

For Maria Mazziotti Gillan, who's always in my corner
And in memory of my mother, who refused to let me be a goner

To my uncle Fernando Medina, Jr., in celebration of his 70th year! —T.M.

This book is livicated to I mighty sons, "with whom I am well pleased."
Through this artwork I honor the man, Berhane Selassie, who carried
the message of justice and unity from the depth of the ghetto to the height
of global consciousness. —J.J.W.

Acknowledgement

Big up to our editor Jennifer Fox and to Kerriann Thompson, my Jamaican sistah. —T.M.

About the Title

The "I and I" in the title is, like Bob himself, multifaceted. It is a way of referring to oneself, yet it means more than simply "I." "I and I" can refer to the unity of God (whom Bob's Rastafarian religion calls Jah) and every human—meaning God is within all of us and we are all one people, equal under him. In Jamaican grammar, "I and I" can also mean "we" instead of merely "I." It discourages thinking of oneself solely as an individual but instead as part of a community. —T.M.

Author's Sources

Booker, Cedella Marley, and Anthony C. Winkler. *Bob Marley, My Son.* Lanham, MD: Taylor Trade Publishing, 2003.

Dolan, Sean. *Bob Marley.* Black Americans of Achievement series. Philadelphia: Chelsea House, 1996.

Farley, Christopher John. *Before the Legend: The Rise of Bob Marley.* New York: Amistad/HarperCollins, 2006.

Gilfoyle, Millie. *Bob Marley.* They Died Too Young series. Philadelphia: Chelsea House, 2000.

Haskins, James. *One Love, One Heart: A History of Reggae.* New York: Hyperion, 2002.

Marley, Cedella, and Gerald Housman. *The Boy From Nine Miles: The Early Life of Bob Marley.* Charlottesville, VA: Hampton Roads Publishing, 2002.

Marley, Rita, and Hettie Jones. *No Woman No Cry: My Life with Bob Marley.* New York: Hyperion, 2004.

Mendell, Jo, and Charles Chabot. *Bob Marley and the Wailers: The Bob Marley Story.* Island Visual Arts, 1991. (videocassette)

Sheehan, Sean. *Jamaica.* Cultures of the World series. Tarrytown, NY: Marshall Cavendish, 2000.

Talamon, Bruce W. *Bob Marley: Spirit Dancer.* New York: W.W. Norton, 1994.

White, Timothy. *Catch a Fire: The Life of Bob Marley.* New York: Owl Books/Henry Holt, 2001.

Text copyright © 2009 by Tony Medina
Illustrations copyright © 2009 by Jesse Joshua Watson

Manufactured in China by Jade Productions

Book design by Kimi Weart
Book production by The Kids at Our House

The text is set in Bell Gothic
The illustrations are rendered in acrylic on illustration board

(HC) 10 9 8 7 6 5 4 3 2
(PB) 10 9 8 7 6 5
First Edition

Library of Congress Cataloging-in-Publication Data
Medina, Tony.
I and I : Bob Marley / by Tony Medina ; illustrated by Jesse Joshua Watson. — 1st ed.
p. cm.
Includes bibliographical references.
Summary: "A biography in verse about the Jamaican reggae musician Bob Marley, offering an overview of key events and themes in his life, including his biracial heritage, Rastafarian beliefs, and love of music. End notes on poems provide further biographical information"—Provided by publisher.
ISBN 978-1-60060-257-3 (hardcover : alk. paper)
ISBN 978-1-62014-030-7 (paperback)
1. Marley, Bob—Juvenile literature. 2. Singers—Jamaica—Biography—Juvenile literature. 3. Reggae musicians—Jamaica—Biography—Juvenile literature.
I. Watson, Jesse Joshua, ill. II. Title.
ML3930.M315M44 2009
782.421646092—dc22   [B]   2008033485

Bob Marley's music is known throughout the world. On classroom visits, when I mention his name, some children are unfamiliar with it. But when I start singing the lyrics "Don't worry about a thing," they suddenly come alive with recognition and happily sing along, "'cause every little thing is gonna be alright!" This call-and-response moment, with Marley's song "Three Little Birds," is inspirational and uplifting. It shows how we are connected by the universal compassion of Bob Marley's timeless message of hope.

I first heard Bob Marley's music as a youngster. The beauty of the beats and the power of his words captivated me. They spoke to that compassion in my heart for the homeless people I encountered riding the New York City subways with my father from the Bronx to Manhattan each Saturday on my way to acting classes.

When he was a boy, Bob Marley fell in love with music and dreamed of becoming a singer and musician. He didn't let the fact that his mother couldn't afford to buy him instruments prevent him from following his dream. He used his imagination and made a guitar from a big old sardine can, a bamboo stick, and electric wire. This wasn't the extent of Bob's curious mind. Throughout his life, he observed people in Jamaica and all over the world—their stories and their struggles. What Bob discovered would greatly affect the kind of artist he would become and the songs he would write and sing.

Bob Marley was a messenger—a poet-musician in the tradition of the West African griot, who passes on the history of his people and comments on current events through storytelling and song. *I and I, Bob Marley* celebrates his remarkable life in that griot storytelling tradition. Poems and notes provide a broader biographical portrait of this amazing man and the light he shared with the world. His musical legacy is a unifying force, inspiring us not only to dance to the beat, but to overcome strife and live together as one.

—Tony Medina

griot (GREE-oh): a traveling poet, storyteller, or musician who shares oral or tribal histories

I Am the Boy from Nine Miles

I am the boy
From Nine Miles

The one sing
Like three little birds
From my mum mum belly

Come to bring
My message

Of Love Love
        Love

In many styles
Roots   Rock
Reggae   Ska

With a heart
Like an angel
With doctor bird wings

And songs in my belly
I have to sing

I am the boy
From Nine Miles

The one kissed
By three little birds
As a baby chile

The one sing
Like three little birds
From my mum mum belly

I am the boy
From Nine Miles

Come share
My message

Stay awhile

My Heart the Island

Mama just a caramel country girl shy as can be
And Papa many many years older than she

Papa is a white man so I've been told
My face a map of Africa in Europe's hold

My heart the island where he and she both meet
Jamaican sand under hooves in a hurried swirl

Papa in a captain's uniform all neat
Ride off on a horse the color of a pearl

Leave Mama and me alone to scrape and fuss
Granpapa house us on his farm of Nine Miles dust

Teach me to plant and care for goats like I'm grown
And when I learn to read palms I look at my own

Wonder where oh where my papa go and roam
Wonder when oh when my papa come back home

Palm Reader

Just a boy of five
I see the future

Buzzing in the palms
Of people's hands
Like a beehive

Tracing lifelines like
Rings on the stump
Of a tree

I feel their future
Humming through me
Like music whirling in me

Granpapa Omeriah says
I am like him

A duppy ghost conqueror
A bad spirit-fighting healer
A tuff gong seer

Spotting bad spirits
At the roots of cotton trees

Chasing wicked ghosts from
Bamboo thickets

Chasing the obeahman
From our homeland

As I work in Granpapa's store
People come to me to
Read their palms

Mama says I'm special
She says I'm charmed
Like a prophet from the Bible

I just sit and smile
Glad to be her chile
Glad she's in *my* future

When My Papa Sends for Me

The day I left my Nine Miles
My mother said don't cry chile
But I cry a hurricane of pain

She gets me ready in my church clothes
Puts me on the bungo-bungo bus to go
To a school to learn what I do not know

   'Cause my papa sends for me
   'Cause my papa sends for me

Wriggling through grimy Kingston streets
With its crowded skinny spaces
And strange strange faces

On the bungo-bungo bus of steel
With its rickety seats and wheels
That squeak and clink and squeal

   Like cranky crickets and lazy frogs
   Potbelly pigs and hungry dogs

Tears bust out of my face
Like a bubble bursting cloud of rain
On my way to a strange strange place

When my papa sends for me
The day my papa the stranger
Sends for me

In Kingston

Papa leaves me with an old white lady
Who's so sick she can't take care of me
She says Papa has to go to work
But he never comes back for me

When I sleep I have the same bad dream
Papa without a face riding away on his horse
While Mama cries and cries 'cause she can't find me

Mornings I wake but don't go to school
I shop and cook and clean Mrs. Grey's old house
That smells like a musty mop from rainwater
Dripping through the roof

When I go out to the market along the busy street
I see people with no bed for sleep or food to eat
Begging for change from a beanie man
Trying to get me to buy his tomatoes
And potatoes with his songs

His music grabs me like a fisherman's hook
Staying in my mind like a good dream
And every time I go by I smile like to say hello
Until he calls me over and teaches me to sing

Please Mister, won't you touch me tomato
Touch me pumpkin an' me potato

When Papa leaves me I am just six years old
And when Mama finally finds me
I am good and fat and seven
She grabs me and hugs me and
Covers my face with a sweet spray of kisses
Taking me back to my Nine Miles heaven

At home in the kitchen while Mama
Heats up the stove with her smile
I bang on pots and pans like drums
And sing

Please Mama, won't you pass me a tomato
Pass me a pumpkin an' a potato

Trenchtown

Old Trenchtown in Kingston
Over the sewers of Babylon

Pressed against concrete walls
In rickety shacks the rain attacks

Thin tin roofs like bullets from Heaven
Like hard bread from Heaven

Skinny chickens and haggard hens
Run across dirt floors

Covered with dead roaches
No green grass or running water

No toilet but what a man
Digs like trenches in Trenchtown

Old Trenchtown in Kingston
Where rude boys roam the streets

Robbin' and a-fightin'
And old men play cards and dominoes

And pretty girls stroll along the yard
While little boys play soccer

With a plastic bucket for a ball
Trenchtown is a poor town

Old Trenchtown in Kingston
Where my hopes hang

On a clothesline where music twirls
From a beat-up radio calling me to sing

Like those three little birds
Outside my window greeting me

Oh Trenchtown my old town
In Kingston in Kingston

At Fourteen

Mama fears I'll be swallowed up by the streets
She doesn't want me hanging around rude boys
With no direction and no way home

She thinks I'll be led into all kinds of trouble
I tell her I follow my own beat
Music will get me out of the rubble

Of Trenchtown streets where dreams are killed
By cops and creeps who want to drag you down
Into the sewers of this rough scuffling town

Mama doesn't want me running the streets
She wants me to stay in school and get a job
To escape this hard-time ghetto life

I tell Mama I want to sing
Babylon school is not my thing
Music is my well of knowledge

At the Queens Theater Talent Show
I win five dollars for how good I sing
Imitating the American singers I hear on the radio

James Brown Nat King Cole Fats Domino
Little Richard Sam Cooke The Moonglows
The Impressions and *The Drifters*—my all-time favorites

The way they comb their hair the stylish clothes they wear
Their voices singing in perfect harmony like rain
Showers me in a waterfall of inspiration

Soon I hook up with Bunny Livingston
And Joe Higgs a singer who lives behind my yard
Who mentors us in his makeshift reggae college

Where I learn how to sing in harmony
And music becomes my way of life
My business and my main source of knowledge

Peter Tosh comes with his own guitar
And each night he, Bunny, and me wail and wail
Into the blue blackness of the sky like shooting stars

Wailing Wailers

Hanging out on the yard
In Trenchtown in Kingston
Listening to other people's radios

Blues, jazz, and R&B along with
Doo-wop ditties and jumping Jamaican ska
Blaring and bouncing along clotheslines

Hypnotizing us with electric beats
Making me want to skank dance
And play chop-chop guitar riffs

While the band wails on
Along a brassy sassy sound
So smooth and sweet

In this day and age
The only way out of the
Hardship of the hood

And its never-ending rage
Is to play soccer
Which we love

Or to do something against
The law and risk a police baton
Whack across the jaw

We don't want to
Land in jail
All we want to do is wail

Be the voice of the voiceless
Bring some happiness and
Consciousness to the down-pressed

Through our redemption songs

Pitch-Black Sky

At night
When I stare
Out into the
Pitch-black
Sky
I see the
Face
Of God
I know as Jah
The Most High

When I stare
Into that dark
Expanse beyond
The stars
I see Africa
With her back
Full of scars

When I hear
The blues man's
Moans wailing
Through the radio
I hear a slave ship
Screaming
My people down below

I come from all
Of this
And there's much
More I need
To know

I want to make songs
As pure and clear
As water
To help my people
Grow

Underneath a Plum Tree

Underneath a plum tree
I and I meet the I-Threes

One of them stands out
With eyes that shout out

To the hurricane in my heart
To the loneliness in my heart

Underneath a plum tree
I and I spot a girl raised
On cornmeal porridge

With *The Lord's Prayer*
In her heart
And a voice full of courage

Underneath a plum tree
I and I hear a girl sing

Voice sweet as the ocean breeze
Voice strong as a tornado unleashed

Swirl in my soul like a top to spin
Lift my soul like a monsoon wind

Beat a blue ska electric rhythm
From my heart to my feet

Voice shake up the sand
Beneath Trenchtown concrete

Underneath a purple plum tree
Moonlight dancing through leaves

With yellow blossoms in her hair
Opened like skirts atwirl

A girl's voice takes hold of me
A girl's eyes won't let go of me

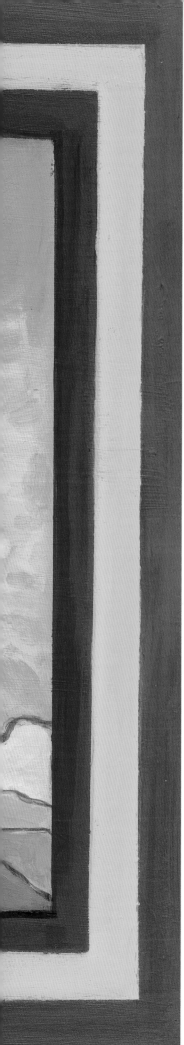

I Am a Rasta Man

A troubadour for the common man
Singing what a Rasta sings

Reggae music from
My guitar strings

Rasta man lyrics
Of peace and love

Rasta man singing
To Jah above

Who came to Jamaica
In human form

Emperor Haile Selassie
Of Ethiopia

Who came to my island
Like a quiet storm

Like Marcus Garvey
He makes us proud

To be Africans shining
In the darkest cloud

I am a Rasta man
A troubadour for every man

Singing what a Rasta sings
One love one heart one song

Singing from the Most High
Put down the weapons and let war die

End all foolish wars that harm
Return to the land of creation—Zion

My songs like a Rasta bible
Written in the heart

Reggae music a Rasta's
Highest art

Island Song

Yell-ow green and black
I want to take
My island back

Yell-ow green and black
I want to take
My island back

From the duppy baldheads
Come to Jamaica
On a pirate ship

Christopher Columbus
And all his men
Turn them to the sea
Again

Yell-ow green black and red
I and I a natty dread

African Arawak Taino
I am from
Slave ship mountains
And Caribbean rum

Port-of-call parish
Trenchtown sewers
Under shacks
In Kingston

Reggae music
Spring out the sand
Buried in concrete
By a wicked hand

Feel the rhythm
Like the ocean
Kissed by the sun

Jamaica Jamaica
Is the one

Indian African
Chinese and
European
All together
To survive

When one man takes
Another man dies

Yell-ow green and black
I want to take
My island back

Yell-ow green and black
I want to take
My island back

Each note I play
Each song I sing
Freedom coming
From my guitar string

Reggae

The King's English
  Turned upside down

Maroons, slaves seeking
  Higher ground

Hungry children playing
  In a shantytown

Me and my girl Rita
  In the dance hall partying

Down down down
  To a rock steady rhythm

And slow ska beat
  On the dance floor

Rita shake her hips
  I and I light step my feet

Raggedy rude boy blue heat
  Drum bass and riddim

Doing the Reggay to
  Toots and the Maytals

The Upsetters, Jimmy Cliff,
  And Lee "Scratch" Perry

The harder they come or fall
  Praying a fight don't break out

And me and Rita don't have to
  Crawl toward the door

Music churning and turning
  Turning and burning

Beats so Skatalite sweet
  Do the Reggay Do the Reggay

With hardly no room
  In this skankin' place

And sweat beads
  Shining up I and I face

That's glistening while we
  Dancing and listening

To songs with hypnotic effect
  We sufferers we shufflers

Party to the music
  Of our hopes and dreams

Chantin' down Babylon
  All night long

Till the morning come
  Till the rooster's song is sung

Music Takes Me

From simmering shantytown
    Shacks of Trenchtown

To the freed streets of Zimbabwe
    I am hurled

And hailed a Reggae king
    With truth as my crown

When the streets of my Jamaica
    Threaten war

I join hand-in-hand
    Fighting politicians in peace

My songs cry out that
    Black blood shall spill no more

And that African unity
    Must increase

War is a cancer that turns
    Everything upside down

Love is the answer
　　Where peace is found

Music takes me
　　All over this world

To New Zealand where I'm
　　Honored by Maori dreads

At home in my Rasta words
　　That sing, *Don't give up the fight!*

To London Paris Dublin and Milan
　　Where hundreds of thousands

Dance together in one love one peace
　　To the rhythm of reggae's heartbeat

Sharing my message and my sound
　　Music and love where peace is found

Hope Road

Music comes to me like birds knocking on my window
Filling me with songs in a nest of love singing at my window

I greet it with words that in my mind roam free and in my heart
Find home like a windswept leaf scratching along my window

Music is a big old rusty sardine can I turn into a guitar
A dream I grab onto like a star shining outside my window

It's a winding road of hope a guava tree shading a sweaty toad
A cool summer breeze twirling the skirt of my window

Music is a joyful noise that opens my heart like a flower
A lightbulb in my mind bright as a flame flickering in my window

When I don't feel like much and frown like a toy in the rain
Gone to rust music is a ray of sunlight smiling through my window

Music is the road I take to the well of hope with its endless spring of
Birds whistling like children laughing and playing beneath my window

Song in My Heart

I am the boy
   From Nine Miles

The one sing
   Like three little birds
      In a reggae style

The one blessed
   By Jah
      To travel miles

Across the world
   With my island girl
      Guitar in hand

And my dreads
   Atwirl

With music
   In my belly

And songs
   In my heart

Healing the world
   With my reggae art

Keeping you always
   Like a song
      In my heart

Notes for I and I, Bob Marley

I Am the Boy From Nine Miles

Nesta Robert Marley was born to Captain Norval Sinclair Marley and Cedella Malcolm on February 6, 1945, in the village of Nine Miles in the St. Ann parish of Jamaica. Legend says that three little birds perched on the windowsill singing sweetly to the newborn baby. Cedella felt this was a sign that her son was blessed by God, that he would grow up to do great things. Confused about the first name Bob's father had given him—it sounded like Lester to her—Cedella later learned that Nesta meant "messenger." Still, her son became known as Robert Nesta Marley, or simply Bob Marley.

My Heart the Island

Bob's parents came from two different worlds that were joined together through Jamaica's history of imperialism and oppression. Jamaica was colonized by Great Britain in 1655 and did not gain full independence until 1962. Bob's father was a sixty-three-year-old white British man. While working as a superintendent of crown lands in St. Ann, Captain Marley often stayed in the house of Katherine Malcolm, Cedella's grandmother. Eighteen-year-old Cedella would see Captain Marley riding around on a white horse as she helped her father, Omeriah, work his land. Captain Marley and Cedella eventually developed a secret relationship. When it was discovered, Cedella's father, who was friendly with the captain, was shocked and disheartened. Omeriah later accepted the relationship on the condition that they marry, which they did. Not long after their son was born, Captain Marley abandoned Bob and Cedella and went to live and work in Kingston, Jamaica's capital. Cedella raised Bob with support from Omeriah, who became the boy's father figure.

Bob was ashamed of his background. He considered his parentage a slave story—a white aristocratic man taking advantage of a young black woman. Because of his light skin and European features, Bob also struggled with discrimination from dark-skinned Jamaicans, who questioned his African ancestry.

Palm Reader

As a child Bob was thought to have special gifts. He was considered a messenger and a seer, a person who could predict events. When Bob was five years old he worked at his grandfather's store reading palms. The customers believed Bob could tell their futures.

Omeriah was an important man in Nine Miles. He owned acres of farmland and a couple of shops. He was also a myalman, an herbalist, or root man, who knew the secrets of natural healing and chasing away evil spirits. Omeriah's faith was based in Jamaican spirituality, a unique blend of European Christianity and African belief systems, emphasizing the supernatural and fear of spirits. Some of these bad spirits were known as duppies (ghosts), and the myalmen were called upon to get rid of them. Obeahmen, on the other hand, were sorcerers who exploited the power of duppies to do harm and influence events. Obeahmen were thought to steal people's spirits, bringing illness or death, whereas myalmen recaptured souls, restoring the spirits of the sick.

When Bob was six months old he became deathly ill. Fearing for her son's life, Cedella called for Omeriah. When he arrived, he knew an evil spirit was overtaking his grandchild. Omeriah used his skills and powers as a myalman to heal Bob. After a few days, the baby was back to normal health.

Omeriah's spiritual beliefs as well as his love of music (he played the organ, fiddle, and banjo) were a great influence on Bob. Cedella, a Christian who sang in a church choir, also fostered her son's early spirituality and love of music.

When My Papa Sends for Me

Captain Marley sent for his son when Bob was six years old. His father decided Bob should live in Kingston in order to receive a better education than he would in Nine Miles. Bob did not want to leave his mother and grandfather and move to a strange place. Nevertheless, he was placed on the bungo-bungo (country bumpkin) bus that transported people from rural areas to the commercial center of the island. Bob had never left the safe confines of his grandfather's farm, and this sudden separation caused him to burst into tears. On the trip to Kingston, his eyes feasted on a landscape of rural pastoral beauty, followed by the stark reality of inner-city poverty. These early impressions had a profound effect on the songs he later wrote and sang.

In Kingston

Once Bob arrived in Kingston, his father took him to live with Mrs. Grey, an elderly white woman who lived in a musty one-room house with a roof that leaked when it rained. She suffered from diabetes and was so frail that she could hardly take care of herself, let alone six-year-old Bob. Bob became Mrs. Grey's errand boy. He cooked, cleaned, and went to the market to buy groceries, and never actually attended school. Cedella was not informed of her son's exact location or how to contact him.

During this time, Bob missed his mother greatly. In a strange place without a mother or father, Bob often had nightmares while he slept. He soon adapted, however, making friends with neighborhood youths and finding things that filled him with wonder on his frequent trips to the market. On one such visit Bob was attracted by the singing of a higgler (street vendor) who performed a special folk song to attract customers to purchase his vegetables. This song had a big impact on Bob. He began repeating it and soon made up his mind that he wanted to become a singer.

After a year of not knowing how to find her son, Cedella was contacted by an acquaintance who had spotted Bob at the market. He had asked the woman to tell his mother to come get him. An exchange of letters vaguely confirmed Bob's location, and his mother was able to find him and take him back to Nine Miles. She noticed that Bob had grown in height and weight over the year, and had matured a great deal as well. Back in Omeriah's market, when asked to read palms, seven-year-old Bob refused, saying, "I'm a singer."

Trenchtown

When Bob was ten years old his mother remarried. She and Bob moved to Kingston with her new husband, Thaddius "Toddy" Livingston, and his eight-year-old son, Bunny. They lived in Trenchtown, a ghetto area built over a sewage drain and noted for its shantytowns and subsidized "government yard" apartments. These dwellings had little greenery and were infested with cockroaches; but housing outside the government yards was even worse, with no running water. Trenchtown was a rough area. It had poor schools, and crime was common. Bob and Bunny did not like Trenchtown at first and could not understand why they had moved there. Still, they quickly adjusted to the dynamic environment that pulsed with social and political upheaval. It was in this tough, vibrant atmosphere that Bob developed a sense of belonging. He learned to play dominoes and soccer. He also learned to fight and swear. In Trenchtown, young males were usually thought to be rude boys (hoodlums) and were constantly being chased by the police.

Since there was little hope of escaping the hardship of ghetto life, many youths succumbed to the streets. Other escapes included playing soccer and singing. The music scene in Trenchtown transfixed Bob and Bunny. They listened to music from old, beat-up radios hanging from clotheslines. Jamaica had evolved its own musical forms, and some local artists were played; but mostly the radio broadcast blues and R&B (rhythm and blues) songs from the United States. In this environment, the teenage Bob and Bunny were inspired to make their own music.

At Fourteen

By age fourteen Bob wanted to drop out of school. He was bored and felt his calling was to make music. He wanted to spend all his time writing and recording. At first Cedella was reluctant. She feared Bob would get caught up in the street life and end up dead or in prison. Eventually, however, she agreed to let him quit school. When Bob was seventeen years old, Cedella helped him get a job as a welder's apprentice. He didn't want the job. It didn't pay well, and it distracted from his music. But in the end Bob took the job to satisfy his mother. Shortly after he began working, a sliver of metal nearly blinded Bob in one eye. That was the end of his welding days.

Bob began to devote himself to his music full-time. He met a well-known Jamaican singer and Rastafarian, Joe Higgs, who lived behind Bob's yard. Joe Higgs was a well-regarded musician who had recorded his own songs, and he also mentored young Jamaican singers in an informal music college. Under Higgs's tutelage, Bob learned to sing in harmony and began to play the guitar. Bunny, Peter Tosh (another young singer), and Bob formed a band—the Wailing Wailers. A wailer is a person who cries out against abuse, injustice, and oppression as a form of resistance. Wailer is also a slang expression for a person who can sing well, who can wail.

Wailing Wailers

Bob, Bunny (who later became known as Bunny Wailer), and Peter shared a love of blues, jazz, and R&B music. The three spent countless hours together in the government yards of Trenchtown listening to music and practicing their own songs. Under Joe Higgs's guidance, they honed their act until they were ready to record. Higgs introduced the group to Clement "Sir Coxsone" Dodd, a well-known local performer and record producer who owned his own studio, Studio One. The Wailing Wailers recorded several singles with Dodd and became very popular in Jamaica after their songs were played on the radio.

Pitch-Black Sky

Influenced by his grandfather and mother, as well as by social and political conditions in Jamaica, Bob's worldview continued to expand. He adopted the Rastafarian religion, with its belief in Jah (God) and extreme pride in African history and ancestry. Slavery, a very painful part of that history, had a direct and profound effect on the conditions of many poor, oppressed Jamaicans. On the streets, in government, and through music, people expressed their anger, discontent, and frustration with the injustices imposed on them for so many centuries.

Bob felt compelled to be a voice for the voiceless, to make revolutionary change through his music. He studied books, newspapers, magazines, and the Bible. He discussed history, politics, religion, philosophy, and social issues with fellow Rastafarians. These activities stimulated the growth of his spiritual and political beliefs and informed his work. Bob's mission to elevate and defend the people of Jamaica naturally extended to a defense and celebration of the island itself. His love of Jamaica's natural beauty began in his youth in the lush, rural village of Nine Miles. As an adult, Bob frequently explored the island with his friends on morning jogs, stopping to bathe in waterfalls and eat fruit from the trees. Bob's deep love for his island and his people led to many great, inspiring songs.

Underneath a Plum Tree

Music brought Bob and his future wife, Rita Anderson, together. The Wailing Wailers recorded their first songs at Clement Dodd's Studio One. The studio was on Brentford Road in Trenchtown near where Rita lived with her aunt Viola. Their yard had a plum tree and was directly across from the Calvary Cemetery for Jamaica's Catholic citizens. Rita spent a lot of time in her yard with her cousin Constantine (nicknamed Dream) and best friend, Marlene. Rita also loved to sing. At the age of ten her aunt had coaxed her into singing on a radio talent show. Rita sang "The Lord's Prayer" and wowed the audience, winning the contest.

When Rita learned that the Wailing Wailers passed by her house on the way to the studio, she convinced Dream and Marlene, who sang with her, to help her get the band's attention. Rita watched and waved at the musicians as they walked to the studio. During a break from rehearsal, Peter Tosh went to meet Rita, Dream, and Marlene. When he found out they could sing, he introduced them to Dodd, who hired the young women as a backup group called the Soulettes, later known as the I-Threes.

Rita, a young single mother, was attracted to Bob but found him to be very shy and quiet. Bob seemed to be interested in Rita too. Dodd noticed the attraction Rita and Bob had for each other. He hired Bob to train and rehearse the Soulettes/I-Threes. One night after rehearsals Bob sent a note to Rita through Bunny, expressing his feelings for her. From that day on Bob and Rita were inseparable. Not long after they began dating, Bob decided to move temporarily to Wilmington, Delaware, to find work. His mother had relocated there, and Bob hoped to make enough money to buy recording equipment. Before he left, Bob and Rita married.

I Am a Rasta Man

Rastafarianism is a religion, way of life, and social movement that emerged in Jamaica in the 1930s. Historically, Jamaica had a mixture of religions from European, African, and indigenous Arawak Indian traditions. During the 1920s, the roots of Rastafarianism began to take hold in the impoverished Jamaican ghettos. Rastafarianism was initially inspired by the black consciousness and back-to-Africa ideas, writings, and speeches of the Jamaican leader Marcus Garvey. He once prophesied the coming of a black messiah when he told his people, "Look to Africa when a black king shall be crowned; he shall be your redeemer." The Bible also referred to Ethiopia as an "earthly paradise." On November 2, 1930, Ras Tafari Makonnen (1892–1975) was crowned emperor of Ethiopia. He became known as Haile Selassie I. His followers considered him to be the embodiment of God on Earth, a black Messiah who had come to redeem and free the black race. It was believed Selassie would return the sons and daughters of Africa to Ethiopia, their promised land, and lead them away from Babylon, the corrupt Western society that historically enslaved and oppressed them.

Poor Jamaicans were attracted to Rastafarianism because of its messages of black empowerment and equality. When Haile Selassie I visited Jamaica in April 1966, one hundred thousand Jamaicans came out to see him. Although Rastafarianism does not have a formal organization and varies in customs, the main tenets are the understanding that Haile Selassie I is God and that Africa is the real home of the black race, a paradise on Earth. Rastafarians often wear their hair in dreadlocks and try to eat an ital (strict vegetarian) diet. Rastafarian language is based on Jamaican patois and is expressed most powerfully through reggae music.

Bob Marley emerged as one of the Rastafarian movement's primary prophets and ambassadors. His music evolved to give Rastafarianism, as well as the plight of impoverished Jamaicans and oppressed people all over the world, a universal appeal and importance. The Rasta phrase "One Love, One Heart," included in one of Bob's most famous songs, came from Marcus Garvey's slogan "One Aim, One God, One Destiny," expressing ideas of universal love, peace, and unity.

Island Song

Jamaica was formed seventy million years ago from volcanic eruptions that also created parts of Mexico and Central America. The island was originally populated by Arawak Indians, who called it Xaymaica. Spanish invaders called it Santiago, but the British, who were the last to colonize the island, called it Jamaica.

Jamaica's history of colonization began on May 5, 1494, when Christopher Columbus and his conquistadors claimed the land for Spain. The Spanish ruled the island for one hundred fifty years, subjugating the Arawak Indians who had lived on the island for eight centuries and forcing them into labor. By 1515, due largely to disease and harsh labor conditions, there were so few Arawaks left that the Spanish began importing enslaved Africans to replace their workforce. In 1655 a British army of seven thousand landed in

Jamaica, putting an end to Spanish colonial rule. The British became the island's new colonizers and overseers of slaves. Sugar and rum—made from distilled sugar—were major commodities of the time, and a huge labor force was required to work the cane fields on sugar estates. Jamaica became a main auction center where slaves were sold to work on local sugar plantations or in other colonies.

African resistance to slavery in Jamaica emerged in the form of the Maroons. Maroon comes from the Spanish word cimarrón, meaning "wild and untamed," but Maroon commonly means "runaway slave." Many of these former slaves did not in fact run away, but had been released by the conquered Spanish settlers. The Maroons took to the mountains and rough terrain to launch guerilla warfare against the English. The slave trade was eventually abolished in 1807, but real freedom for the slaves did not emerge until after a rebellion in 1838. Colonization, oppression, and struggle left indelible marks on Jamaica's history and people. Bob Marley rose from this turbulent history to become known as "the voice of the people," fighting against oppression with his music.

Reggae

Before reggae reigned supreme in Jamaica, its musical predecessor—known as rock steady—began making a splash on the island. The Wailers recorded a number of rock steady songs at Dodd's Studio One. Rock steady was a refined Jamaican sound rooted in American soul and doo-wop. The music of Jamaican youths, it expressed the problems, fears, and attitudes of Jamaica's underclass, celebrating and glamorizing the island's rude boys and ghetto heroes.

Reggae emerged in the late 1960s. Like the island that gave birth to it, reggae has roots that are African, European, and indigenous. It is most closely related to Jamaican ska music, a combination of R&B and mento (Jamaican folk) music. R&B music introduced the organ and electric guitar into the bass-dominated reggae sound, while reggae rhythms are based on African Nyahbinghi drumming (used in authentic Rastafarian music). Reggae lyrics feature social, political, and historical commentary. It is music from the streets of Kingston, reflecting the dissatisfaction of Jamaican youths, who felt disregarded by society.

Toots and the Maytals first officially used the term reggae in their song, "Do the Reggay." But the word has a number of possible origins. It could have come from the patois word streggae which means "rudeness" or "rude-boy." Or, according to Toots, from streggay, a term used to refer to a very attractive woman. Reggae can also mean "quarrel," as well as "regular" (down to earth).

Reggae music was rarely played on Jamaican radio stations because of its strong political content. However, with its heavy Rastafarian influence, it also stressed ideas of peace, love, and equality. It wasn't until reggae songs became popular in London, England, that reggae began to gain worldwide appeal. In addition to Toots and the Maytals, some of reggae's first stars were Lee "Scratch" Perry, Desmond Dekker, and Jimmy Cliff, whose role in the film The Harder They Come also helped put reggae music on the map. With his great talent as a musician and songwriter, and his political and ethical vision, Bob Marley eventually emerged as reggae's premiere superstar and iconic figure. He once said, "My music fight against the system. My music defend righteousness."

Music Takes Me

In June 1976 political unrest broke out on the streets of Jamaica between warring political parties. The governor-general declared a state of emergency. Bob was asked by Michael Manley's People's National Party (PNP) to perform at an outdoor concert called "Smile Jamaica." Bob had openly supported Manley's democratic socialist party in the previous national elections because it emphasized various social programs to alleviate the suffering of Jamaica's poor. Still, Bob did not want to perform on behalf of any politicians. Assured the concert was promoting peace, not any political party, Bob agreed to perform.

Hired thugs representing Edward Seaga's opposing Jamaican Labour Party (JLP) warned Bob against performing at the concert and even threatened his life. Following the death threats, Bob was assigned protection at his home and studio at 56 Hope Road by an armed vigilante group of the PNP (known as the Echo Squad). A week before the concert, armed men arrived at Bob's house on Hope Road and opened fire. Bob, his wife Rita, and his manager, Don Taylor, were injured but survived. Rita was shot in the head, and Bob was shot in the arm. Mysteriously, the guards hired to protect Bob were nowhere to be found. The day of the concert Bob still showed up to perform, creating a tremendous stir of surprise and excitement among the more than fifty thousand concertgoers.

In spring 1978, Jamaica was once again gripped in political violence. The tension was so severe that there was threat of a civil war. Bob was asked to perform at the "One Love Peace Concert," organized by Jamaica's two rival political parties. Bob accepted. At the concert he famously joined the two rival political candidates' hands together in an act of peace and unity. This groundbreaking moment in Jamaican political history earned Bob the United Nations Medal of Peace.

Bob toured all over the world with his music, traveling to the United States, Europe, Australia, Japan, and Africa. In 1980, Bob was invited to perform at the official Zimbabwe Independence Day ceremony, celebrating the end of white colonial rule in the country formerly known as Rhodesia. Bob Marley became reggae music's ambassador, spreading his message of peace, justice, and equality wherever he went.

Fate Opens Up Its Hand

Since childhood, soccer (called football in Jamaica and other parts of the world) was one of Bob Marley's greatest passions. Whenever he was on the road with his band, he always made time for a game between shows. Soccer was a way for Bob to relax, relieve stress, and stay fit. During a friendly game in Paris in 1977, Bob's right foot was injured. The nail on one of his toes was torn off. He continued performing throughout his European tour, but his toe would not heal. After shows, Bob often found blood in his boot. A London doctor diagnosed the toe as cancerous and told Bob to have it amputated so the cancer would not spread. Because of his Rastafarian beliefs, which considered the body a temple and forbade the cutting of one's flesh, Bob refused to follow the doctor's suggestion. Instead, he sought alternative treatment in the form of a skin graft followed by bed rest.

On September 21, 1980, the morning after a performance at Madison Square Garden in New York City, Bob went jogging with some friends. During the run he collapsed to the ground, convulsing. The cancer in Bob's toe had spread throughout his body; he was diagnosed with a brain tumor and given only three weeks to live. Bob traveled to Bavaria seeking emergency treatment from a controversial German oncologist, but it was too late. He returned to his mother's home in Miami, Florida, and on May 11, 1981, Bob Marley, reggae's greatest star, succumbed to cancer. He was just thirty-six years old when he died. Back in 1969, Bob's friend Dion Wilson from Wilmington, Delaware, remarked that Bob would become rich and famous and live a long life. Bob turned to him and said, with great confidence, "Oh no. I'm going to die at thirty-six." This was to become a prophecy fulfilled, an ominous indication of Bob Marley's visionary powers.

Hope Road

56 Hope Road was the address of Bob Marley's mansion and studio. He had risen to such stardom and success that he purchased the home to make it the studio for his Tuff Gong record company. Many of Bob's Rastafarian brethren thought the house was too big for Bob and felt as if he had moved away from his roots. But Bob's doors were always open, and people from all over were welcomed. In fact, it was rumored that Bob was supporting hundreds of Jamaicans with the money from his internationally acclaimed music career.

Bob also had eleven children: three with his wife, Rita Marley, and seven out of wedlock. He adopted Rita's first child, Sharon, who was born before they met in 1965. A number of his children have carried on his musical legacy and become well-regarded musicians. Ziggy, Damian, Julian, and Ky-Mani Marley have all recorded contemporary reggae songs.

No matter how hectic things got at 56 Hope Road, Bob still managed to make time for his primary passion—making music. Although many of his songs speak out against economic oppression, political repression, and the unnecessary violence of war, they are also filled with a love of humanity and hope for a better future. At 56 Hope Road Bob was able to fulfill his destiny as a messenger, the one announced like a sign of hope by three little birds at his window upon his birth.

Song in My Heart

Bob Marley emerged from the rural farmland of Nine Miles and the government yard shantytowns of Trenchtown to become one of the most important musicians the world has ever known. His music propelled reggae and Rastafarianism onto the international stage and made political songs as popular as love songs. He was Jamaica's foremost ambassador of reggae and considered a true prophet. He championed the plight of the poor and oppressed of his native Jamaica and beyond, directly involving himself in political issues at home and abroad. Bob once said, "My music will last forever." His songs, with their messages of peace and love, are a legacy to the world, living on for generations.